THIS IS WHY WE PRAY

THIS IS WHY WE PRAY

A Story About Islam, Salah, and Dua

Ameenah Muhammad-Diggins

Illustrations by Aaliya Jaleel

callisto
publishing
an imprint of Sourcebooks

Published by Callisto Publishing LLC C/O Sourcebooks LLC
P.O. Box 4410, Naperville, Illinois 60567-4410
(630) 961-3900
callistopublishing.com

This product conforms to all applicable CPSC and CPSIA standards.

Source of Production: Wing King Tong Paper Products Co.Ltd. Shenzhen, Guangdong Province, China
Date of Production: November 2023
Run Number: 5035638

Printed and bound in China.
WKT 13

Contents

A Letter to Grown-ups vi
A Letter to Kids vii

Chapter 1
THE FIVE PILLARS 1
What Are the Five Pillars? 3

Chapter 2
OFFERING SALAH 15
Why Does Allah Ask Us to Pray? 17
How Do We Get Ready to Pray? 18
How Do We Pray? 22

Chapter 3
MAKING DUA 33
What is Dua? 35
Being Grateful 36
Talking to Allah 38

On Your Way! 43
Extra Duas and Prayers 44
Glossary 49
Resources 52

A Letter to Grown-ups

Dear Grown-ups,

I'm excited that you have chosen this book for the little persons in your life. Fostering love and understanding of Islam is the best gift we can give the next generation. Writing this book has been a source of joy and trepidation. It was an undertaking I did not approach lightly.

As a parent and an educator, I am committed to helping our children foster a personal connection to Allah. It is my desire to present the Five Pillars, salah, and dua in a way that helps young readers find joy in worshipping Allah. While religious memorization is good, it is equally important for children to be active thinkers as a way to get closer to Allah.

This book is written as a story, in hopes of opening up a beautiful dialogue between grown-ups and little ones reading it. I encourage you to read the story with your children, allow them to engage with it, and help them complete the activities at the end of each chapter. May this book aid you in developing lifelong memories rooted in the love of Allah and Prophet Muhammad (ﷺ).

Your sister in Islam,
Ameenah Muhammad-Diggins

A Letter to Kids

Dear Reader,

Isn't it exciting to get a new book? One great thing about a book is that you can read it over and over. Each time, it becomes more special.

I pray you will love this book and that it will help you live a life full of happiness and joy. This book tells a special story, because it is all about building a bond with Allah. Allah is the creator of everything. He cares for you and me and gives us all we need.

You can read the story alone or with the help of a grown-up. Be sure to ask your family or teachers if you have questions. There are fun things to do at the end of each chapter to begin your own adventure getting to know Allah.

Put on your listening ears and your adventure cap. Put your hand over your heart and give it a tap. Now that you have your book, get comfy in a nice reading nook. The story is about to begin . . . let's jump in!

With love,
Auntie Ameenah

CHAPTER 1

✴ THE FIVE PILLARS ✴

The Five Pillars of Islam are important beliefs that every Muslim learns. We use them as a guide to help us live a good life. In this book, we will learn about the Five Pillars with a little help from the Abdur-Rahman family: a young girl named Aliya; her brother, Amar; and their mama and papa. The Abdur-Rahmans live on a quiet street in a home filled with lots of love. Aliya and Amar are going to learn all about the pillars of Islam—just like you.

WHAT ARE THE FIVE PILLARS?

The Abdur-Rahman family loves spending time together. They play different games every week. Papa loves board games. Mama loves card games. Aliya and Amar both like guessing games. Today, they are playing a question game.

Papa makes a drumroll sound, and Mama asks one last question: "There are five things in Islam that every Muslim believes. They are called the Five Pillars of Islam. Do you remember what they are?"

Aliya raises her hand first. "**Shahada**, **salah**, **zakat**, **siyam**, and the last one is **Hajj**," she says.

"Ding, ding, ding!" Papa says, smiling as Aliya skips around the living room.

Mama cheers for Aliya. She got every pillar right! Then Mama takes a moment to remind Aliya and Amar what each pillar means.

The first pillar, shahada, is to say there is only one God and that the Prophet Muhammad (ﷺ) was His last Messenger.

The second pillar is salah. Five times a day, we stand before Allah to pray.

The third pillar is pretty awesome: zakat, giving charity to help people in need.

The fourth is siyam, or fasting. We fast during the month of **Ramadan** each year. We also do extra good deeds like giving to others. When the sun is up, we do not eat.

The fifth pillar of Islam is Hajj, a journey to the holy city of Mecca. We visit an important place called the **Kaaba** and perform the rituals started by Prophet Ibrahim (عليه السلام).

"All right, you two," Mama says. "Let's clean up and get ready for bed. We have a big day tomorrow."

Amar gathers up the game pieces to put them away.

ALLAH AND HIS PROPHETS

Amar is too excited to sleep. His family is planning to go to the beach tomorrow, and he can't wait! He's also thinking about what his family said about the Five Pillars of Islam.

Mama taps softly on Amar's door. "Are you ready for bed?" she asks with a smile.

"Yes, Mama, but I have a question," Amar says, sitting up. "How do we know about the Five Pillars?"

Mama sits on the edge of Amar's bed. She loves that her son asks questions, and she wants to help him understand. She tells him that Allah is the creator of everything. He created the sun, the moon, all animals, and all people. Over time, people forgot or changed how to pray to God and how to treat each other.

Because Allah loves us, He sent Prophets and Messengers to guide us. Every group of people was sent a Messenger or Prophet (or someone who was both) to help them. There were many different Prophets, but the final Messenger was Prophet Muhammad (ﷺ).

PRAYING EVERY DAY

"Wake up! It's time for **Fajr**!" Mama calls the next morning.

Aliya and Amar grumble from inside their rooms.

Papa calls them, too. "Remember . . . we go to the beach today!"

Aliya and Amar leap out of bed and rush downstairs. Mama shakes her head and smiles. "Why didn't I see this much excitement when I said it was time to pray?"

Mama motions for the children to sit beside her. "You know how we wash our hands so that our bodies stay healthy? Salah does that for our hearts. Allah made us. He knows that sometimes we forget everything he has given us, and our connection to Him can get muddy. Allah made salah so that our connection to Him stays healthy and clean."

There are five prayers spread out during the day, as a reminder that Allah is always with us. Each salah is like a special gift. We pray Fajr before the sun rises early in the morning. **Dhuhr** is in the early afternoon around lunchtime. **Asr** is later in the afternoon. **Maghrib** is around sunset. **Ishaa** is the last prayer of the day, usually right around your bedtime.

GIVING TO OTHERS

Together, the family packs the car for beach day. They put in towels, toys, and food to take to the beach. Before they leave, Mama grabs a few extra meals to take to their neighbor Mrs. Washington. Aliya and Mama make their way across the street to their neighbor's house, carrying the food in their arms. Mrs. Washington has recently come home from the hospital. Mama and some of the other families on their street offered to cook meals until she was feeling better.

After dropping off the food, Aliya climbs into the car. "It felt good to help our neighbor," she says.

"Helping the community is an important part of being a Muslim," said Papa. "Allah has told us that the best people are the ones who help other people. Part of being a good person is caring about others."

FASTING DURING RAMADAN

Papa starts the car. It's time to hit the road! Aliya can't wait to build sandcastles with her cousin Bashirah. Amar is excited to collect seashells. Papa is looking forward to seeing his brother Sharif and hitting the waves.

Amar buckles his seat belt. "I want to hear about Uncle Sharif's Ramadan journey!" he says.

"Hajj journey, buddy, not Ramadan journey," Papa says, correcting him.

Amar giggles at his own mistake. "What is Ramadan again, Papa?"

"It's the month when we fast during the day," Aliya says.

Papa smiles. Aliya is right. "Along with siyam, Ramadan is also when we give extra charity and go to the **masjid** for **iftar**."

Aliya remembers going to pray at their local masjid and eating a meal after sunset during Ramadan last year. It was good to see the other people from their community during such a special time.

Ramadan is the month when the holy book of the **Quran** was revealed to Prophet Muhammad (ﷺ) a long time ago. It is a special month for Muslims. We fast during the day if we are not sick or traveling. Each day during Ramadan, we are strengthening our relationship with Allah. It's like training for the rest of the year and a reminder to stay grateful to Allah for His blessings.

TRAVELING FOR HAJJ

After a car ride filled with sing-alongs, road trip games, and many questions from Amar, Papa pulls into the beach parking lot. Uncle Sharif and Bashirah are already there.

The children scramble out of the car. Aliya and Bashirah twirl in their matching beach skirts. Amar gives his uncle a big hug and a high five.

Papa and Uncle Sharif pitch the beach tent. Everyone finds a good place for their beach blankets.

"What was Hajj like?" Amar asks after the family is settled.

"**Subhan Allah**," Uncle Sharif says, praising Allah as he remembers his life-changing journey. "There were millions of Muslims from all over the world. Old, young, rich, poor—all coming together as one Muslim family to complete the fifth pillar of Islam. We followed the steps of Prophet Ibrahim (ﷺ), his wife Hajar, and his son Prophet Ismail (ﷺ). We walked around the Kaaba. On the most important day of Hajj, we prayed and made **dua** on Mount Arafat. Every Muslim adult who is able should go to Hajj at least once. I feel like a new person!"

"Wow, that sounds amazing," Amar says. "I can't wait to go!"

Quran Story Time

Have you ever had trouble tying your shoes? Or maybe you fell and scraped your knee? Maybe you got sad and gave up when you couldn't figure out a puzzle.

Do you think it is silly to ask Allah for His help for something that seems small? Did you know Allah loves when we talk to Him, no matter how big or small we think our problem is?

Prophet Muhammad (ﷺ) told us to ask for Allah's help with all of our needs, even something as small as a broken shoelace.

Anas ibn Malik reported: The Messenger of Allah, peace and blessings be upon him, said, "Let one of you ask his Lord for his needs, ALL OF THEM, even for a shoestring when his breaks." (Sunan al-Tirmidhi)

When My servants ask you [O Prophet] about Me: I am truly near. I respond to one's prayer when they call upon Me. So let them respond [with obedience] to Me and believe in Me, so that they may be rightly guided. (Surah Baqarah 2:186)

WHAT CAN WE DO TOGETHER?

There are so many activities you can do as a family or with friends to keep learning about the Five Pillars of Islam! Here are a few ideas to help you get started.

1. Make up a song or poem to help you remember the Five Pillars of Islam.

2. Help start a Ramadan and **Eid** family tradition. Maybe you can break your fast with something special on Fridays, or you can all wear the same color on Eid. What can you do to make Ramadan and Eid special for your family?

3. Learn the steps of Hajj and put on a play about it for family or your local masjid.

4. Help your community. Organize or take part in a community cleanup day.

5. Be a good neighbor. Do something nice for one of your neighbors, like bake cookies or make a homemade gift just for them.

WHAT DO YOU THINK?

You've already learned so much about the Five Pillars! Try talking to your family or teachers about what you learned. Ask them questions about things you want to learn more about.

Aliya and her mother made food for their neighbor who wasn't feeling well. How do you think that made their neighbor feel?

Why do you think it is important for Muslims to be active in their communities?

Has anyone ever done something nice for you or your family? How did that make you feel?

CHAPTER 2

OFFERING SALAH

In this chapter we will learn about the second pillar of Islam, salah. We will also learn why it is important to pray our five daily prayers. Throughout the chapter there are tips for making salah something you are excited to do every day. There will also be ideas for activities you can do with your family and friends to continue to learn.

WHY DOES ALLAH ASK US TO PRAY?

Everyone is having a wonderful time at the beach. Aliya and Bashirah are building a sandcastle. Amar chases the water back and forth along the shore. Papa and Uncle Sharif are jumping waves in the ocean. After a while, Mama tells everyone to come back to their picnic blanket for salah.

"Even at the beach? We're having so much fun," Aliya says.

"Yes, even when we're having so much fun!" Papa replies. Papa explains that Allah made everything on the beach they were enjoying. He created the sun, sand, ocean—and their family! It's important to pause for salah wherever you are, to thank Allah.

Salah allows us to show our love for Allah. On good days, it is easy to be thankful. But we also make salah even when we are grumpy or sad. Those are some of the best times to be close to Allah. Just like how your parents love to hug you when you are happy *and* to make you feel better when you are sad, Allah loves it whenever we take time to talk to Him.

Imagine that these moments to pause and pray are special times to talk to our creator. It is a gift to have time every day to talk to Allah!

> **Tip:** Plan your day around salah. It is easier to worship Allah when you know what time each prayer is. Ask a grown-up to help you look up salah times, and try not to plan activities then.

HOW DO WE GET READY TO PRAY?

Papa finds a quiet area near a sand dune where the family can pray. But before they talk to Allah, they have to clean themselves. Papa picks up a fresh water bottle for **wudu**.

"Wudu is when we wash ourselves before salah," he tells Aliya and Amar. "Just like we should find a clean and tidy place to pray, we should also clean ourselves before we talk to Allah."

Papa tells the kids each step of wudu.

1. Say "Bismillah" before starting. This means "in the name of Allah." It helps us remember that we are cleaning ourselves to get ready to pray.

2. Wash your hands in water three times.

3. Wash your mouth three times. Swish the water around in your mouth and then spit it out.

4. Wash your nose three times using your right hand.

5. Wash your whole face three times.

6. Wash your right arm all the way up to the elbow three times.

7. Wash your left arm all the way up to the elbow three times.

8. Wipe water over your head once.

9. Wipe water over your ears once.

10. Wash your right foot up to the ankle three times.

11. Wash your left foot up to the ankle three times.

Mama smiles as the family finishes wudu. She helps Aliya fix her scarf for salah. Just like we want to have clean bodies, we also want to look nice when we talk to Allah. We should try not to wear dirty clothes. Girls should cover their hair and body, and boys should make sure their pants go down to their knees.

Tip: Look your best. If you were to meet a queen or president, you would want to look nice. When we make salah, we are standing in front of Allah, the king of everyone on earth! Pick out a special outfit to wear just for salah. It can be as fancy as you want, so you'll look great and feel excited to talk to Allah.

HOW DO WE PRAY?

Papa calls the **adhan**, the Muslim call to prayer. It lets everyone know that in a few minutes it will be time to pray. In some cities the adhan is called through speakers outside the masjid. After the adhan comes the **iqamah**. The iqamah is called right before prayers begin. During the iqamah, worshippers stand ready to begin salah. The family gathers behind Papa.

"Allahu Akbar," Papa calls, beginning the prayer.

> **Tip:** Keep a prayer rug with you. Ask a grown-up to keep a prayer rug in the car, or pack one in your bag. Keeping one with you will make sure you always have a clean place to pray.

1. We first begin with our **niyyah**—our intention. We say with our heart that we plan to make salah. We clear our minds of everything except wanting to follow what Allah tells us.

2. Raise your hands to your ears and say "Allahu Akbar." This means "Allah is the Greatest." He is more important than anything we were busy with before it was time to pray.

3. Put your hands over your heart and say the seven verses of Surah al-Fatihah, the first chapter of the Quran. This is the most important **surah** of all. When we say this surah, we tell Allah how great He is because He created the world. We also tell Allah that we only pray to Him, just like in the first pillar of Islam.

4. Say any other short surah you know. This is when you get to choose anything from the Quran!

5. Say "Allahu Akbar" again. Bow down and put your hands on your knees. This is called going into **ruku**. When you are in ruku, say "Subhaana Rabbee al-Adheem" three times. This means "Allah is perfect."

6. Say "Allahu Akbar" and stand back up. We say this throughout our prayer to keep reminding ourselves how great Allah is.

7. Put your hands up to your ears and say "Allahu Akbar." Sit down and put your forehead and hands on the floor. This is called going into **sujud**. While you are in sujud, say "Subhaana Rabbee al-A'laa" three times. This means we are thankful for Allah's mighty power over everything. When your head is down like this, you are as close as you can be to Allah in prayer. When you are still in sujud, make any dua you want.

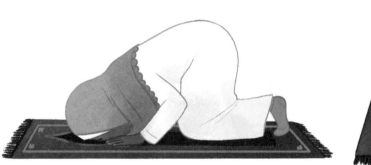
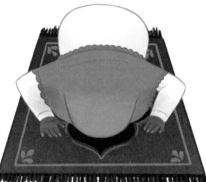

8. Say "Allahu Akbar" and sit up on your knees for a few seconds. Say "Allahu Akbar" again, then put your head back on the floor in sujud. Say "Subhaana Rabbee al-A'laa" again three times.

9. Say "Allahu Akbar," then stand up. That completes your first time through, or one **rakaah**. Do everything again, all the way from Surah al-Fatihah to sujud, but this time, don't stand up. Stay sitting on the floor, and say:

At Tahiyyaatu lilaahi was Salawaatu wat tayibaatu,

Assalaamu 'alaika ayyuhan nabiyyu wa rahmatul laahi wa barakaatuh,

Assalaamu 'alaynaa wa 'alaa 'ebaadillaahis saaliheen,

Ash hadu allaa ilaah ilallaah Wa ash hadu anna Muhammadan 'abduhuu wa rasuuluh.

This is called **Tashahhud**. Just like with Surah al-Fatihah, we tell Allah that we only pray to Him and that Prophet Muhammad (ﷺ) is His Messenger.

10. Pray each rakaah until you finish the right number for that time of day. Say the Tashahhud after every two rakaat. The Fajr has two rakaat, so you say the Tashahhud once. Dhuhr has four rakaat. Asr has four. Maghrib has three, and Ishaa has four rakaat. That means you say the Tashahhud two times in each of those prayers.

After the second Tashahhud, say:

Allahumma Salli Ala Muhammad wa Ala Ali Muhammad, Kama Sallayta Ala Ibrahima Wa ala Ali Ibrahima innaka Hameedum Majeed

Allahumma Barik Ala Muhammad wa Ala Ali Muhammad, Kama Barakta Ala Ibrahima Wa ala Ali Ibrahima innaka Hameedum Majeed.

This is a dua for Prophet Muhammad, Prophet Ibrahim (علیه السلام), and their families.

11. After finishing your last rakaah, turn your head to the right. Say, "Assalamu alaikum wa rahmatu Allah." Then, turn your head to the left and say it again. This is called **Tasleem**.

After the Tasleem, salah is finished!

Tip: Pick a spot to focus on. Sometimes it's easy to get distracted when we pray. To help you pay attention, try picking a spot on your prayer mat to look at while you pray.

Once they finish their salah, Papa tells Aliya and Amar that it is important not to rush through prayers. Sometimes you may want to pray fast so you can get back to playing. But salah is the most important part of our day. We should always give our salah our full attention and pray with our whole heart.

Papa gathers the blanket, and the family walks back to their spot on the beach. Aliya and Amar settle under the beach umbrella and unwrap their lunch.

"It felt nice to stop to pray," Aliya says between bites.

"That was pretty cool," Amar agrees, sitting down to eat his sandwich.

Quran Story Time

Allah tells us that reciting the Quran at Fajr is very special. While other people are sleeping, we wake up for Fajr and pray with our whole hearts. Allah sees us and is happy. He promises us that waking up early in the morning to read Quran and pray Fajr gives us a special reward from Him.

> **Establish Prayer from the declining of the sun to the darkness of the night; and hold fast to the recitation of the Quran at dawn, for the recitation of the Quran at dawn is witnessed . . . and during the night wake up and pray, as an extra offering on your own, so that your Lord may raise you to a highly praised status. (Surah al-Israa 17:78–79)**

Sometimes it can be hard to wake up so early and still use your whole heart to pray. The more you do it, the easier it will become. When your parent says you're ready, try waking up for Fajr one day. How did you feel knowing that Allah was rewarding you even when it was more difficult to wake up?

WHAT CAN WE DO TOGETHER?

Here are some fun activities you can do with family and friends to keep learning.

1. Decorate a salah space in your home. Ask if it can be a family project. Add lights and beautiful pillows and scarves to make it special.

2. Still learning the parts of salah? Make a chart where you can color in each part after you learn a step. Celebrate with your family after all the parts are colored in.

3. Get a pen pal. What is your favorite part of salah? Write a letter to a friend or family member telling them all about what you love about salah.

4. Make a nighttime routine. Go to bed at a good time every night so it will be easier to wake up for Fajr. Ask your family to pray together in the morning so you can support each other.

WHAT DO YOU THINK?

You've just learned a lot about salah! Try talking to your family or teachers about what you just read. Ask them questions about salah. Here are a few to get you started.

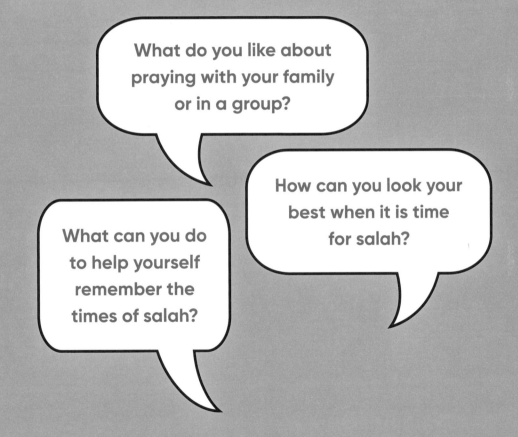

What do you like about praying with your family or in a group?

How can you look your best when it is time for salah?

What can you do to help yourself remember the times of salah?

CHAPTER 3

✸ MAKING DUA ✸

Did you know we can talk to Allah any time we want? Yes, Allah loves when we ask Him for help! We don't have to wait until it is time for salah. When we talk to Allah outside of salah, that is called making dua.

WHAT IS DUA?

Papa drives into the masjid's parking lot just in time.

"I thought we were going to be late for Islamic school!" Aliya says.

"I thought so, too," Papa says, laughing. "I made dua and asked Allah to help us be on time. **Alhamdulillah**, He answered my dua!" He helps the children out of the car.

Aliya walks into her classroom. On the chalkboard in big letters is the word "dua." She tells her teacher how they were just talking about dua before class. Sister Lubna is so impressed! She asks if Aliya can explain it to the class.

"Dua is a connection straight to Allah," Aliya says. "It's when we ask Allah for something, like forgiveness or favors. We can make dua anytime, like before bed or when we are scared. Allah loves when we talk to Him, so we should try to make dua as much as we can."

"That is very good," says Sister Lubna. "Prophet Muhammad, peace be upon him, said one of the best ways to pray is by making dua. When we ask Allah for help, we become closer to Him."

During salah, you read surahs from the Quran in Arabic. But Sister Lubna tells the class how we can talk to Allah in any language that is easy for us. The most important part is knowing that Allah hears us and will answer in a way that is best for us.

BEING GRATEFUL

"I can't find it anywhere!" Amar cries after Islamic school, searching for his favorite toy. Papa and Aliya help him look all around the car. It isn't under the seat, and it isn't in the trunk. Amar wants them to go back to the masjid to look for it there, but they are almost home.

Amar is very upset about losing his favorite toy.

"It's hard to lose things we love," Papa says. "Did you know that if we thank Allah even when we are upset, He gives us more to be thankful for?"

Amar sits quietly, remembering what he has that makes him happy. *Thank You, Allah, for all of my other toys and books. Thank You for a fun day at the beach with my family, and our house, and yummy food.* He thanks Allah for everything he can think of. Slowly, he begins to feel better.

Quran Story Time

One day a long time ago, Prophet Muhammad (ﷺ) was walking in the desert and saw an old woman struggling to carry something heavy. He asked if he could help her. She said yes, so he picked up her bags and asked where she was going. The old woman said she was leaving town because she had heard there was a man named Muhammad who was saying all sorts of bad things and dividing the town. She went on to talk badly about the Prophet, not knowing he was the kind man helping her. Prophet Muhammad listened and did not interrupt her or try to defend himself. The old woman was impressed with the young man helping her and saw how his face lit up when he smiled. When they arrived at her destination, she asked for his name so she could thank him. The Prophet told her that he was the same person who had made her leave town. The woman was shocked! She couldn't believe that the man she had been talking badly about was the same man helping her. She said that such a kind and helpful person could not be wrong. She became a Muslim because of Prophet Muhammad's kindness.

This is a great lesson on kindness and gratitude. Can you think of a time in your life when you were grateful that someone did something kind for you?

TALKING TO ALLAH

Amar feels better after thinking about the things that make him happy. But he is still a little sad about losing his favorite toy. He prays to find his toy, but he doesn't find it.

"What do you do when you make dua but don't get what you want?" Amar asks Mama.

"That's a good question," Mama says. "You know how sometimes you ask to have cupcakes for breakfast? I always give you something better for you, like fruit or oatmeal. Sometimes, your duas are like that, too."

Mama explains that we may not always get exactly what we ask of Allah. Instead, Allah gives us something better. Our job is to never lose hope, and to keep talking to Allah and asking Him for help. Allah always answers us, no matter what.

Talk to Allah about whatever is in your heart, whenever you want. Before you go to sleep and when you wake up are great times to make dua. Allah never gets tired of helping us.

The Prophet Muhammad (ﷺ) told us there are things we can do to always stay connected to Allah. We should thank Allah as soon as we wake up. We should also remember to feel grateful in our hearts. There are many duas we can say throughout the day, but the best duas are the ones that fill our hearts with joy when we say them. No matter what you say, dua is your personal time to talk to Allah.

Mama puts her arms around Amar and Aliya. "Did you know that Allah is our protector? Just like our good friends, Allah does not get tired of helping us."

When we thank Allah even when things don't go as we hoped, we tell Him that we trust Him. We know that Allah has given us many wonderful things, even when things are hard. All we have to do is trust Him.

WHAT CAN WE DO TOGETHER?

Here are some fun ways to make dua with your family or friends.

1. Ask to create a family dua. Each family member can add to it to make it special.

2. Make a "Thank You, Allah" gratitude journal. Write down your special prayers and things you thank Allah for. Keeping a dua journal is a fun way to look back at how much Allah has blessed you with.

3. Memorize duas. The Prophet Muhammad (ﷺ) taught us many different duas. Try to memorize a new one every week. Some easy duas to learn are for when we wake up, before we eat or go to the bathroom, and before we put on our clothes. Remember, you can say a dua in any language that is easy for you.

4. Talk about your day. Pick a time during the day, like during dinner, and take turns with your family remembering all of the good things that happened that day. If your day was hard, still try to find five things to be grateful for.

WHAT DO YOU THINK?

You've just learned about dua and how to talk to Allah every day. Try talking to your family or teachers about what you learned. Here are a few ideas to get you started.

What are some things you are grateful for?

What are some things you would like to ask Allah for?

Was there a time you were disappointed about something? What would you tell Allah about that time?

On Your Way!

Look how far you've come! I am proud of you for learning so much about Islam. Give a grown-up in your life a big hug. Thank them for sharing this book with you.

Amar, Aliya, and YOU have had a good time learning new things. Remember to be kind to others, help people in your community, and talk to Allah every day.

My dua for you is that you always carry Allah with you in your heart. Remember, Allah wants the best for you. He loves when we talk to Him and thank Him. I hope you are excited to make salah and dua every day! The more we remember Allah, the more He blesses us. Now let's say "Alhamdullilah!"

Extra Duas and Prayers

Sometimes we feel sad and our hearts become filled with fear. No need to worry—Allah is always near. There are many duas we can say. They help us stay close to Allah and reward us with an amazing day.

1. When You Don't Feel Well

Did you know that you can say Surah al-Fatihah even when you are not in salah? It is a special dua that keeps us safe and protects us. Prophet Muhammad (ﷺ) said it is the greatest surah in the Quran. When you are scared or are feeling sick, recite Surah al-Fatihah with your heart.

بِسْمِ اللهِ الرَّحْمنِ الرَّحِيمِ

الْحَمْدُ للّهِ رَبِّ الْعَالَمِينَ

الرَّحْمـنِ الرَّحِيمِ

مَالِكِ يَوْمِ الدِّينِ

إِيَّاكَ نَعْبُدُ وإِيَّاكَ نَسْتَعِينُ

اهدِنــا الصِّرَاطَ المُستَقِيمَ

صِرَاطَ الَّذِينَ أنعَمتَ عَلَيهِمْ
غَيرِ المَغضُوبِ عَلَيهِمْ وَلاَ الضَّالِّينَ

Bismillah-ir-rahman-ir-rahim

Al-hamdu li-llah-i rabb-il-'Alimin

Ar-rahman-ir-rahim

Malik-i yaum-id-din

Iyaka na'budu wa iyaka nasta'in

Ihdi-na-s-sirat al-mustaqim

Sirat alladhina an'amta 'alayhim

Ghayr il-maghdub-i 'alayhim

Wa la adh-dhalin

In the name of God, the Lord of Mercy, the Giver of Mercy!

Praise belongs to God, Lord of the Worlds,

The Lord of Mercy, the Giver of Mercy,

Master of the Day of Judgment.

It is You we worship; it is You we ask for help.

Guide us to the straight path:

The path of those You have blessed

Those who incur no anger

And who have not gone astray.

—Surah al-Fatihah 1:1–7

2. When You Wake Up

Before we get out of bed, the first thing we should do is thank Allah. We thank Allah that He gave us the gift to wake up and live a beautiful day. Here is a dua to say in the morning.

اَلْحَمْدُ لِلَّهِ الَّذِي عَافَانِي فِي جَسَدِي، وَرَدَّ عَلَيَّ رُوحِي، وَأَذِنَ لِي بِذِكْرِهِ.

Alhamdu lillahil-lathee 'afanee fee jasadee, waradda 'alayya roohee, wa-athina lee bithikrih.

All praise is for Allah, who restored to me my health and returned my soul and has allowed me to remember Him.

—At-Tirmidhi 5:473

3. To Feel Safe

Prophet Muhammad (ﷺ) told us to recite Ayat al-Kursi in the morning and before we go to bed. It is the greatest **ayah**, or verse, in the Quran. It is a reminder of how great Allah is. Ayat al-Kursi reminds us that Allah protects everything and never gets tired of taking care of us.

اللّهُ لاَ إِلَـهَ إِلاَّ هُوَ الْحَيُّ الْقَيُّومُ
لاَ تَأْخُذُهُ سِنَةٌ وَلاَ نَوْمٌ
لَّهُ مَا فِي السَّمَاوَاتِ وَمَا فِي الأَرْضِ
مَن ذَا الَّذِي يَشْفَعُ عِنْدَهُ إِلاَّ بِإِذْنِهِ
يَعْلَمُ مَا بَيْنَ أَيْدِيهِمْ وَمَا خَلْفَهُمْ
وَلاَ يُحِيطُونَ بِشَيْءٍ مِّنْ عِلْمِهِ إِلاَّ بِمَا شَاء
وَسِعَ كُرْسِيُّهُ السَّمَاوَاتِ وَالأَرْضَ
وَلاَ يَؤُودُهُ حِفْظُهُمَا وَهُوَ الْعَلِيُّ الْعَظِيمُ

Allahu laa ilaaha illaa huwal
haiyul qai-yoom; laa taakhuzuhoo
sinatunw wa laa nawm; lahoo
maa fissamaawaati wa maa
fil ard; man zallazee yashfa'u
indahooo illaa be iznih; ya'lamu
maa baina aideehim wa maa
khalfahum; wa laa yuheetoona
beshai 'immin 'ilmihee illa be
maa shaaaa; wasi'a kursiyyuhus
samaa waati wal arda wa la
ya'ooduho hifzuhumaa; wa huwal
aliyyul 'azeem.

Allah, there is no god except Him. He is the Living One, the
All-Sustaining. Neither drowsiness befalls Him nor sleep. To Him
belongs whatever is in the heavens and whatever is on the earth.
Who is it that may intercede with Him except with His permission? He
knows what is before them and what is behind them, and they do
not comprehend anything of His knowledge except what He wishes.
His seat embraces the heavens and the earth and He is not wearied
by their preservation, and He is the All-Exalted, the All-Supreme.

—Surah al-Baqarah 2:255

4. To Stay Healthy and Safe

"Afiyah" is a word that means to be taken care of in all things. For example, if we want to be healthy or safe, we can ask Allah for afiyah with this dua:

اللَّهُمَّ إِنِّ أَسْأَلُكَ الْعَفْوَ وَالْعَافِيَةَ فِي الدُّنْيَا وَالآخِرَة

Allahumma inni as'alukal-'afwa wal-'afiyah fid-dunya wal-akhirah.

O Allah, I ask You for forgiveness and well-being in this world and in the hereafter.

—Sunan Ibn Majah 5:3871

Glossary

adhan: A call to let Muslims know that prayer will start soon. This is a good time to make wudu. Adhan is said before the iqamah.

alhamdulillah: Arabic phrase used to thank Allah. It means "praise be to God."

ayah: A verse or short section in the Quran. Every surah is made up of one or more ayahs.

dua: A prayer that "calls out" to God. Muslims use dua to talk to Allah and ask Him for forgiveness and help.

Eid: A celebration for Muslims all over the world. There are two Eids every year. Eid al-Fitr, which means "festival to break the fast," is at the end of Ramadan. Eid al-Adha means the "festival of the sacrifice" and is after Hajj.

Hajj: The fifth pillar of Islam. It is to travel to Mecca on pilgrimage at least once in your life.

iftar: The meal Muslims eat to break their fast at sunset during the month of Ramadan.

iqamah: A call to let Muslims know prayer is starting now. One should be standing and ready to pray when one hears it. It comes a few minutes after the adhan.

Kaaba: One of the holiest masjids in Islam. It is the cube-shaped building in Mecca that Muslims turn to when they pray.

masjid: An Islamic house of worship, where Muslims can come together to pray.

niyyah: The intention one has when they pray or do something for Allah. People can have good intentions or bad intentions when doing things.

Quran: Islam's holy book. Allah sent ayahs in Arabic to the Prophet Muhammad (ﷺ) so that he could teach people about Islam. All the ayahs and surahs are combined in the Quran.

rakaah (plural **rakaat**): The set of movements and prayers performed by Muslims in salah.

Ramadan: The month in the Islamic calendar when the Quran was originally revealed to Prophet Muhammad (ﷺ). During Ramadan, Muslims fast during the day and do acts of kindness to become closer to God.

ruku: The act of bowing while standing up and putting the hands on the knees during salah.

salah: The second pillar of Islam. It is to pray five times a day in the following order:

   Fajr: sunrise morning prayer with two rakaat

Dhuhr: early afternoon prayer with four rakaat

Asr: late afternoon prayer with four rakaat

Maghrib: sunset prayer with three rakaat

Ishaa: evening prayer with four rakaat

shahada: The first pillar of Islam. It is to pledge there is no god but Allah and that Prophet Muhammad (ﷺ) was His final Messenger.

siyam: The fourth Pillar of Islam. It means fasting, when one does not eat or drink during daylight hours.

Subhan Allah: An Arabic phrase used to say how great Allah is. It means "God is perfect" and "Glory to God."

sujud: The act of bowing with head and hands on the ground during salah.

surah: A chapter in the Quran. The Quran has 114 surahs total!

Tasleem: The last step of salah, when one looks right and then left to finish prayer.

wudu: The Islamic ritual of cleaning parts of the body to prepare for prayer.

zakat: The third pillar of Islam. Muslims who have extra wealth give charity every year to those who need it.

Resources

Here are some fun resources to keep learning more about Islam and what it means to be Muslim.

Websites

Noor Kids

noorkids.com

An educational company all about building confidence in Muslim children. You can sign up for a subscription to books and programs for kids 0–3 and 4–9 years old. The books use cute animal characters to teach character building and critical thinking.

Omar and Hana

omarhana.com

An Islamic cartoon series. The Omar and Hana app offers songs, cartoons, and interactive storybooks. You can also watch videos on their YouTube channel, Omar and Hana.

Muslim Kids TV

muslimkids.tv

Learn about Islam while having fun! This site has more than 5,000 cartoons, games, and activities for kids 2–11 years old.

One4Kids

one4kids.net

One4Kids has a whole bunch of animated films with their famous cartoon character Zaky. Zaky loves teaching kids about Allah and the Prophet Muhammad (ﷺ), and encouraging good character and manners.

Islamic Books for Kids

islamicbooksforkids.com

This online bookstore offers hundreds of books and board games for Muslim kids. They even have crosswords and coloring pages you can download and print out at home.

Books

Bashirah and the Amazing Bean Pie by Ameenah Muhammad-Diggins

Allah Made Everything by Zain Bhikha

The Proudest Blue by Ibtihaj Muhammad

Zaynab's Enchanted Scarf by Robyn Abdusamad

My Kufi by Adil Ismaaeel

Mommy's Khimar by Jamilah Thompkins-Bigelow

The *Ilyas and Duck* series by Omar S. Khawaja

Ramadan Moon by Na'ima B. Robert

I Can Pray Anywhere! by Aisha Ghani

Acknowledgments

Ya Rabb! Inspire me to always be thankful for Your favors which You blessed me and my parents with, and to do good deeds that please You. And instill righteousness in my offspring. I truly repent to You, and I truly submit to Your Will.

—Surah al-Ahqaf 46:15

To my husband, Anwar, and our children, Anwar and Amaya: thank you for encouraging me when I doubted myself, for giving me the time to write and unconditional love, and for being a source of forever joy in my heart and soul.

My parents, Samir Muhammad and Firdows Muhammad, thank you for the greatest gift a parent can bestow upon a child, Islam, and for a childhood filled with love, laughter, and early morning talks after Fajr that molded my sisters and me into the women we are today.

Thank you to my sister Shambra, my first best friend, my number-one cheerleader, and the best big sister in the whole world.

Layla Abdullah-Poulos, for your encouragement and sisterhood, I am forever grateful.

To the entire publishing team that brought *This Is Why We Pray* to life: I am grateful and humbled. Thank you for believing in me.

Forever in gratitude,
Ameenah

About the Author

 **Ameenah Muhammad-Diggins** is an American Muslim author, entrepreneur, and speaker. Her work is inspired by her love of community and her experiences as an African American Muslim growing up in Philadelphia. Her book *Bashirah and the Amazing Bean Pie* made history in 2019 by becoming the first Muslim children's book to be adapted and produced into a stage play by a top ten US children's museum, the Please Touch Museum. Her work has been recognized by *Essence*, the Huffington Post, *Philadelphia*, *SJ Magazine*, *Philadelphia Family*, and an appearance in Dove's self-esteem campaign. Ameenah has helped women self-publish books and start businesses through her online training workshops. Additionally, Ameenah is the founder of Haute and Muslim, an online lifestyle shop for Muslim families. Ameenah currently resides in New Jersey with her husband and their two children.

About the Illustrator

 **Aaliya Jaleel** is a Sri-Lankan American illustrator based in Dallas, Texas, who loves illustrating bright, pastel color palettes and floral themes. Some of her past works include the books *Under My Hijab* and *Muslim Girls Rise*. In addition to being an illustrator, Aaliya also works as a designer for animation.